A little book on MEN

Rahul Roy is an independent documentary filmmaker. Besides directing a number of internationally acclaimed films on the theme of masculinities, he has also written widely on men and gender issues.

Anupama C. Hara is a broadcast animator by profession. She is also an illustrator and an avid painter.

Sherna Dastur is a freelance graphic designer and makes documentary films once in a while. Her film *Manjuben Truck Driver* (2002) received international acclaim.

Sexualities
General Editor: Gautam Bhan

supported by RCSHA, DFID, Unifem, Charca, Save the Children

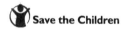

AAKAR
www.southasianmasculinities.org

A

little **book**

On

MEN

by
Rahul Roy

fully illustrated in black, white and gray by
Anupama Chatterjee & Sherna Dastur

YODA PRESS

 YODA PRESS
268 A/C Vasant Kunj
New Delhi 110 070
www.yodapress.com

Published in India
by YODA PRESS

First published 2007
Second impression 2007
Third impression 2009
Fourth impression 2012

ISBN 978 81 903634 8 8

Printed at Chaman Offset Printers, Delhi 110002
Published by Arpita Das for YODA PRESS

Oh I am lost

Some place

Somewhere

From which place

I have no news

Nor can hear

Even

About myself

Ghalib

General Editor's Foreword

When I was fourteen, someone asked me what my caste was. I honestly didn't know. Needless to say, I'm not dalit, because if I was, the option of not knowing—more accurately, not being told, reminded, and made aware of it—would never have existed. The first sign of privilege is always asking, rather than being asked, the questions—never having to self-reflect, and possessing, in a sense, the luxury of ignorance. For many, privilege is often this unconscious, and it is this lack of consciousness and reflection on which any resistance to change is built. In India, this is more true of masculinity than perhaps any of our other identities.

Men don't talk about what it means to be a man. Men, actually, don't talk at all, or, at least, this is what we are constantly told. They just are, as they always have been—strong and silent like the Malboro man who fears nothing and can/must get whatever he wants. Does he have moments of fear? Anxiety? We never see them. Are there days when he doesn't want to be the Malboro Man? Does he have that choice? We don't know. Why does the Malboro Man look the way he does? Is he happy? Does he cry sometimes? Who does he love? Does he love? Do you and I want to be him? These are questions that we men never ask each other, or ourselves. Yet, in our minds, the Malboro Man is firmly implanted as our one guide to masculinity that has no public or visible counter, and he comes in a package with all the extra add-on's: power, violence, silence, sex, strength, and independence.

India today is abuzz about how things are changing for the new Indian woman. Yet no one is talking about men. The furore over metrosexuality—an arguably superficial concept that a friend once described as "a theory with the weight of a passing comment"—dominated cultural conversations for a period of time. To me, the buzz over metrosexuality is important for one thing more than any other—it shows how desperate we are to find ways to talk about men and masculinity. I would go as far as to say that it shows that we are eager to find ways to talk differently about men—not just to dress up the Malboro Man and take him for a pedicure, but to free him, and us, of the rigid confines of his eternal hyper-masculinity.

Gender has remained, largely, about women. For a long time, it has needed to. It is time to break—just as the women's movement did several decades ago—another cycle of silence: the silence about men, men's lives, and masculinities. Masculinity is changing. We have to give it a language. We have to give men a language in which they can talk about and understand themselves in different and individually unique ways, and break the inevitable associations we have with traditional, patriarchal and heterosexual masculinity. We need this to free men in their friendships and relationships with each other and with women.

The Sexualities list at Yoda Press is proud to be part of this new language. This *Little Book on Men* has a big task before it, and it has taken it on admirably. Ideal for practitioners while remaining accessible to the general reader, it is an excellent introduction to the big questions about men and masculinities, one that everyone should give to themselves, or to the men in their lives. Here's to a saner, calmer, less self-destructive, more nuanced, and, in the end, more human Malboro Man (who, hopefully, will also quit smoking all the way).

New Delhi,   **Gautam Bhan**
November 2006

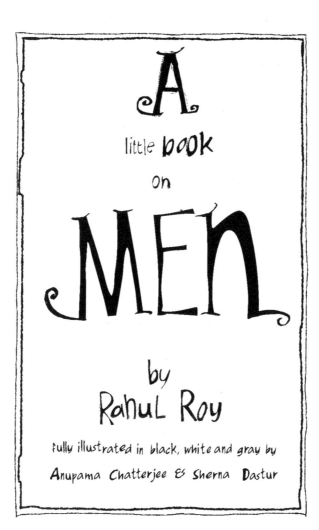

A little book on MEN

by
Rahul Roy

fully illustrated in black, white and gray by
Anupama Chatterjee & Sherna Dastur

with inputs from
Sanjay Shrivastava & Uma Devi

I had to defend myself

```
            Our people were murdered.
You listen to people
            talking about it
and you read about the events.

        All you feel is pain and anger.
```

There would be rioting every day
or every few days

        with people getting shot,
bombs going off in the city regularly.

        We always felt under attack.

        I mean you always waited
                for an incident to happen.

        It was unavoidable
            because of the conditions
            under which we were working.

    The constant humiliation, insults,
        the inhuman treatment...
                it became too much.

I didn't have to sit back and
think about the rights and
wrongs of committing violence.
I felt violence was being done on me.
Everyday we were under attack.
    I had to think it out, how could
    I stop what was happening to my
                brothers and sisters
and then there was no choice.

    I felt pushed against the wall.
        I couldn't respond.
    I was angry.

We were getting it from them,
so we decided we will
take the fight to them

You had to fight
for your religion,
do you understand what I'm saying,
you had to fight
for your identity.
You had to prove that you were men.

Justice Garg to probe violence on Honda Workers

New Delhi, July 26

The Haryana Government today ordered a judicial inquiry after severe criticism of the police "brutality" by parties across the political spectrum.

Terror in Varanasi, nation on alert

GUJARAT'S SHAME

Violence against the minority community continues in Gujarat even as the government sticks to its stand that the situation is under control.

Four farmers killed in police firing while demanding more water for irrigation; anger still brewing

West Bengal, Jharkhand observe shutdown over Kalinga Nagar tribal ...

Woman beaten to death for dowry

Our Correspondents , Ghaziabad, June 1

A young woman was beaten to death for dowry in Shahid Nagar Mohalla of Sahibabad on Saturday night.

Murders and attacks on dalits continue unabated, in UP and in Tamil Nadu.

A brutal assault

The gang rape in Seoni district of Madhya Pradesh, a State that has one of the country's highest crime rates against Dalits, once again points to the community's plight in a caste-ridden society.

Sixty million Indian workers strike against government economic policies

Bloodbath in Orissa

Fisherman killed in police firing in AP, 39 injured

HYDROGEN BOMBS Green

Groping in the dark

Both Chief Minister Sayeed and the Central government have realised that the violence must be contained before talks can replace terror, but neither knows how to go about it.

...nel of Chief Ministers to tackle naxalite violence

...pecial Correspondent

...EW DELHI: A committee of Chief Ministers of naxal violence States will be constituted to initiate and pursue a coordinated approach in tackling the extremist violence and activity.

Task force to keep eye on Naxals

Mumbai, July 26
A special anti-Naxal task force being set up by the Maharashtra Government will look out for sympathisers of the Left-wing extremist groups.

...amp at Jamia to sensitise youth against gender-related violence

...ew Delhi, January 2
...elhi's terrible record in the gory sphere of violence against women is a well ...own though rather ugly fact about the city

Another summer of killings

Militants have renewed their killings in the Kashmir Valley, taking advantage of the reduction in security levels in view of the Kargil conflict.

MUMBAI, JAN. 19. The Nobel Laureate, Shirin Ebadi, deplored the violence against the religious minorities in Gujarat and compared it to the violence which killed Mahatma Gandhi.

Kalinga Nagar firing kills spirit of industrialisation

BHAGAT SINGH THE SAME

India's 500,000 tea workers end strike

KOLKATA: Nearly 500,000 tea workers have ended a strike in the eastern Indian state of West Bengal after unions agreed to accept performance-related pay.

Woman injured in acid attack

3 killed, 75 hurt in Navi Mumbai police firing

Nationwide strike on Sept 29

Honda urges workers to join work

New Delhi, July 25
Trade union activists today staged protest outside the Haryana Bhavan here, protesting against the police cane-charge on workers of Honda Motorcycles and Scooters India Ltd. in Gurgaon.

Almost 1 in 5 married women have experienced domestic violence.

Source: NCRB 1999

Kalinga Nagar tribals reject peace offer; Road blockade continues

Demolitions in Delhi

The United Nations Special Rapporteur on adequate housing has criticised India for demolishing slums in Mumbai and New Delhi.

We live in a world full of conflict and violence. Perhaps the most significant facet of these conflicts is the fact that men are the central actors within this entire spectrum of violence.

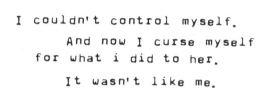

```
I couldn't control myself.
        And now I curse myself
  for what i did to her.
        It wasn't like me.



    At that time I felt
     this was the only option.
         Now I wonder
```

Unequal power structures get articulated in the language of violence. In gender terms, communication is often based on violence, with mostly men having the right to speak.

"Gender based violence is a policing mechanism unleashed to perpetuate gender inequalities and keep in place gendered orders. It is rooted in rigid discourses of what constitutes the masculine and the feminine and the power relationships between men and women."
Alan Greig

Why do men invariably find themselves at the Centre of Violence?

Is it that men are biologically (as some people have argued) 'hard wired' towards violence?

by that logic, are women biologically non-violent?

Amongst the many significant contributions to our understanding of gender was the theoretical and practical assertion by the women's movement in the 1960s that biology could not determine the destiny of women. Since then few have doubted that women have been gendered culturally, historically and situationally. Much of feminist politics and theorising has been around breaking the social and economic subjugation of women. The belief that you can change your destiny has remained central to feminist politics.

Because woman's work is never done and is underpaid or unpaid or boring or repetitious and we're the first to get fired and what we look like is more important than what we do and if we get raped it's our fault and if we get beaten we must have provoked it and if we raise our voices we're nagging bitches and if we enjoy sex we're nymphos and if we don't we're frigid and if we love women it's because we can't get a "real" man and if we ask our doctor too many questions we're neurotic and/or pushy and if we expect childcare we're selfish and if we stand up for our rights we're aggressive and "unfeminine" and if we don't we're typical weak females and if we want to get married we're out to trap a man and if we don't we're unnatural and because we still can't get an adequate safe contraceptive but men can walk on the moon and if we can't cope or don't want a pregnancy we're made to feel guilty about abortion and...for lots and lots of other reasons we are part of the women's liberation movement.

WOMEN'S RIGHTS MANIFESTO, NATIONAL ORGANISATION FOR WOMEN

Betty Friedan has contributed to the reshaping of American attitudes toward women's lives and rights. Through powerful writing and activism, Friedan became the most effective leader of the American Women's Movement.

Friedan's 1963 book, *The Feminine Mystique*, made an enormous impact, triggering a period of change that continues till today.

"The problem that has no name — which is simply the fact that American women are kept from growing to their full human capacities — is taking a far greater toll on the physical and mental health of our country than any known disease."

"Man is not the enemy here, but the fellow victim."

Simone de Beauvoir is best known for her 1949 treatise *Le Deuxième Sexe (The Second Sex)*. As an existentialist, de Beauvoir accepts the principle that existence precedes essence; hence one is not born a woman, but becomes one. Extract from *The Second Sex*:

"But first we must ask: what is a woman? 'Tota mulier in utero', says one, 'woman is a womb'. But in speaking of certain women, connoisseurs declare that they are not women, although they are equipped with a uterus like the rest. All agree in recognising the fact that females exist in the human species; today as always they make up about one half of humanity. And yet we are told that femininity is in danger; we are exhorted to be women, remain women, become women.... But conceptualism has lost ground. The biological and social sciences no longer admit the existence of unchangeably fixed entities that determine given characteristics, such as those ascribed to woman, the Jew, or the Negro."

"What women remain unsure about, however, is whether or not their biology has played a part in making and keeping them the 'second sex'. Such uncertainty is quite understandable in a male-dominated society where not only is history written by those who uphold the status quo but all the sciences are likewise in their hands. Two of these sciences, biology and anthropology, are of prime importance in understanding women and their history. Both are so heavily biased in favor of the male sex that they conceal rather than reveal the true facts about women."

Excerpt from the pamphlet *Is Biology Women's Destiny?* by Evelyn Reed, leader of the Socialist Workers Party and a prominent spokesperson for the women's liberation movement in the late 1960s and early 1970s.

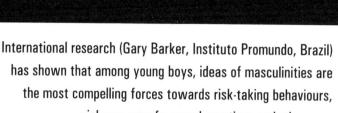

If biology is not destiny, then there must be something behind the gendering process that impels men to take risks, or choose violence as the path to resolve conflict.

International research (Gary Barker, Instituto Promundo, Brazil) has shown that among young boys, ideas of masculinities are the most compelling forces towards risk-taking behaviours, violence, unsafe sexual practices and misogyny.

Are courageous not cowardly

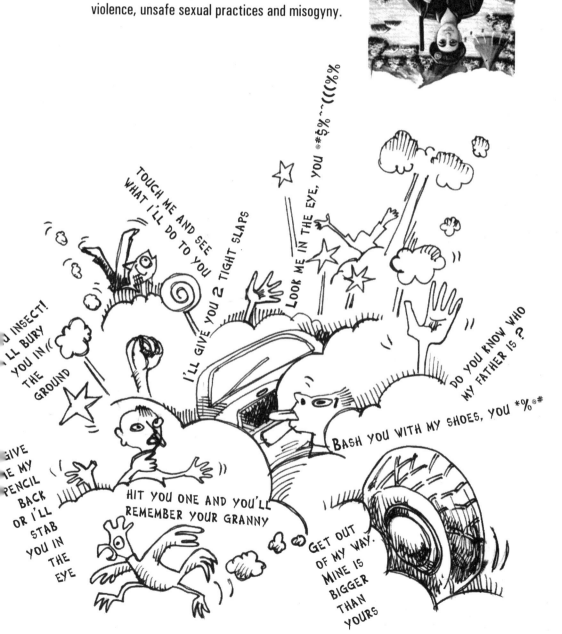

TOUCH ME AND SEE WHAT I'LL DO TO YOU

LOOK ME IN THE EYE, YOU @#$%~~(((%

I'LL GIVE YOU 2 TIGHT SLAPS

INSECT! I'LL BURY YOU IN THE GROUND

DO YOU KNOW WHO MY FATHER IS?

BASH YOU WITH MY SHOES, YOU *%@#

GIVE ME MY PENCIL BACK OR I'LL STAB YOU IN THE EYE

HIT YOU ONE AND YOU'LL REMEMBER YOUR GRANNY

GET OUT OF MY WAY. MINE IS BIGGER THAN YOURS

AN IDEAL
(GOOD HABITS)
आदर्श बाल

Eat well for strong muscles

Protect their sisters

Are not laz

Are team players

Brushes up the teeth

Do n

Have clean and healthy thoughts

Do not take law into hands

Do not tease girls

BOY

Are generous not selfish

Salute parents

Don't complain

Gender is the set of culturally accepted norms of behaviour that are seen as appropriate for the sexes in a given society at a given time.

The sex-gender system is the institutionalised system which allots resources , property and privileges to persons according to culturally defined gender roles.

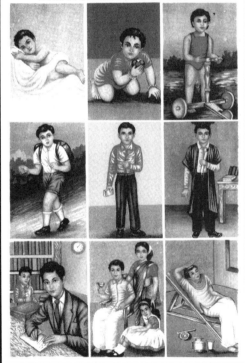

HUMAN STAGES AND DUTIES

Munna holds the television, he has his arms around it.

The screen flickers to life.

A blank screen.

Is he going to fill it with images... his own images...

his dreams?

Ravi dropped out of school and
works as an apprentice in a factory,
learning to make instruments.

Munna and his three friends,
Aman, Tony and Ravi
are walking
through a narrow lane.

Tenements stare at each other,
jostling for some
non-existent space

life spills out
into the narrow lane.

There are old men and women
        fixed to the same spot...
    statues with stories,
            lives lived, still living.

                Munna says he can't breathe in his house,
                        it is suffocating.
        The lane is certainly not wider than his house,
                but yes, it is much longer.

            how much space do you need
    to breathe or to suffocate?

MADHYA PRADESH मध्य प्रदेश

TAMIL NADU तमिलनाडु

UTTAR PRADESH उत्तर प्रदेश

WEST BENGAL पश्चिमी बंगाल

MAHARASHTRA महाराष्ट्र

RAJASTHAN राजस्थान

ORISSA उड़ीसा

SIKKIM सिक्किम

PUNJAB पंजाब

TRIPURA त्रिपुरा

NAGALAND नागालैंड

MEGHALAYA मेघालय

MANIPUR मणिपुर

DELHI दिल्ली

ASSAM असम

BIHAR बिहार

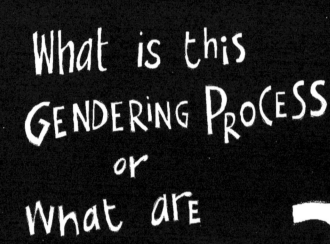

What is this GENDERING PROCESS or What are MASCULINITIES?

Masculinities, the gender
system that makes men,
remains the least researched,
the most unrecognised, the
least visible, pool of darkness
of the South Asian reality.

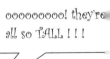
oooooooooo! they're all so TALL !!!

GUJARAT गुजरात

HARYANA हरियाणा

KERALA केरल

KASHMIR कश्मीर

KARNATAKA कर्नाटक

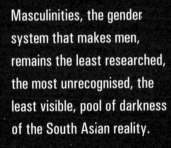
HIMACHAL PRADESH हिमाचल प्रदेश

Women's lives, histories and struggles have seen an upsurge of research and representation but the same cannot be said of men as gendered entities.

We know very little of the mechanics of men's behaviour patterns in different social and life settings. We certainly know the obvious — the visible, hegemonic masculinity that bristles and valourously displays its wares — but what about various other masculinities, those that remain silent, hidden, de-legitimised, disenfranchised, pushed under, often defeated and mostly unrecognised?

"A man would never set out to write a book on the peculiar situation of the human male. But if I wish to define myself, I must first of all say: 'I am a woman'; on this truth must be based all further discussion. A man never begins by presenting himself as an individual of a certain sex; it goes without saying that he is a man."

Simone de Beauvoir

IF Women ARE nOT biOLOGically non-Violent THEN MEN CANNOT BE Biologically VioLent AND IF All men ARE NOT VioLENT then many MEN MUST BE non-violent.

What is the story of these men, these masculinities that shun violence?

How do different forms of masculinities relate to each other? Are they locked in some form of permanent conflict?

Why are some forms of masculinity more assertive and more public?

Are different forms of masculinities definite, unbreakable, permanent or do they change over time?

We can go on and on posing questions that remain largely unanswered.

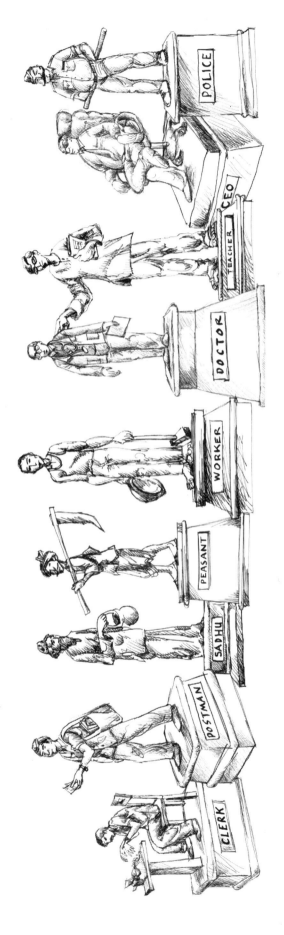

It has been argued that the invisibility of masculinities to men is the dividend they gain from occupying higher positions in the patriarchal pyramid.

The invisibility of gender to men, this zone of silence, is a political space. A space fraught with tensions and conflicts. A space that hides the struggles to become a man, insecurities about the impermanence of manhood, experiences of power and powerlessness, the hard realities of scrounging for work, and conflicts that defy comprehensible resolutions.

put a mirror in his hand — without eyes, what will he see? kabir

As the Chinese proverb has it, the fish are the last to discover the ocean. This was made clear to me in a seminar on feminism I attended in the early 1980s. There, in a discussion between two women, I first confronted this invisibility of gender to men.

During one meeting, a white woman and a black woman were discussing whether all women were, by definition, 'sisters,' because they all had essentially the same experiences and because all women faced a common oppression by men. The white woman asserted that the fact that they were both women bonded them. The black woman disagreed. "When you wake up in the morning and look in the mirror, what do you see?" she asked. "I see a woman," replied the white woman. "That's precisely the problem," responded the black woman. "I see a <u>black</u> woman. To me, race is visible every day, because race is how I am <u>not</u> privileged in our culture. Race is invisible to you, because it's how you are privileged."

Michael Kimmel

DON'T QUESTION ME!

he's a man, he knows how to run the country

i know what i'm doing

i'll take care of it. Leave it to me.

WHAT DO WOMEN WANT?

he 's a man, he knows how to run his family

real men satisfy their women

i'm doing all of this for you. This is my legacy

I need to be more assertive

he's a man, he knows how to handle money

WHY DO I WORK SO HARD TO EARN SO LITTLE

how will i pay for the car

how will I pay for the house

how will I provide for her

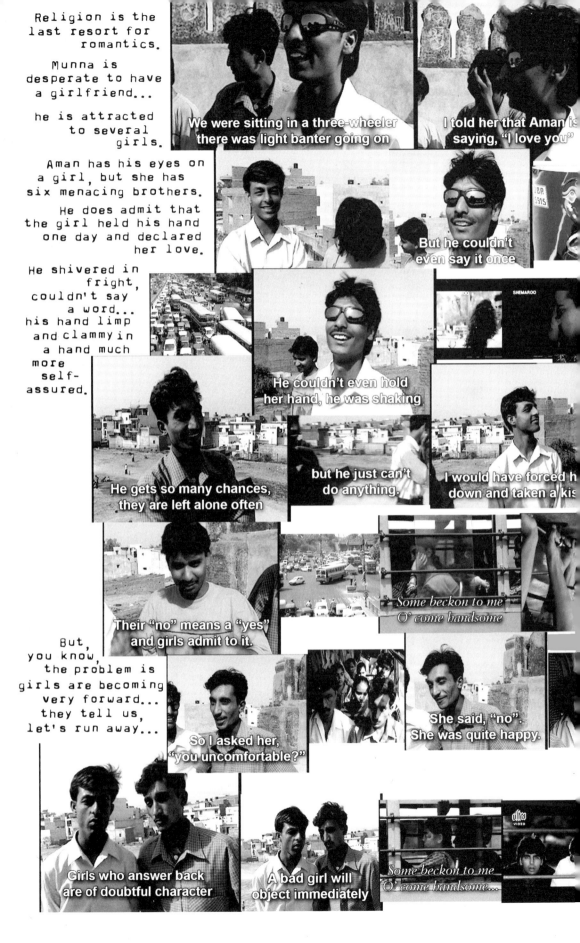

Religion is the last resort for romantics.

Munna is desperate to have a girlfriend...

he is attracted to several girls.

Aman has his eyes on a girl, but she has six menacing brothers.

He does admit that the girl held his hand one day and declared her love.

He shivered in fright, couldn't say a word... his hand limp and clammy in a hand much more self-assured.

But, you know, the problem is girls are becoming very forward... they tell us, let's run away...

We were sitting in a three-wheeler there was light banter going on

I told her that Aman is saying, "I love you"

But he couldn't even say it once

He couldn't even hold her hand, he was shaking

but he just can't do anything.

I would have forced h down and taken a kis

He gets so many chances, they are left alone often

Some beckon to me O' come handsome

Their "no" means a "yes" and girls admit to it.

So I asked her, "you uncomfortable?"

She said, "no". She was quite happy.

Girls who answer back are of doubtful character

A bad girl will object immediately

Some beckon to me O' come handsome...

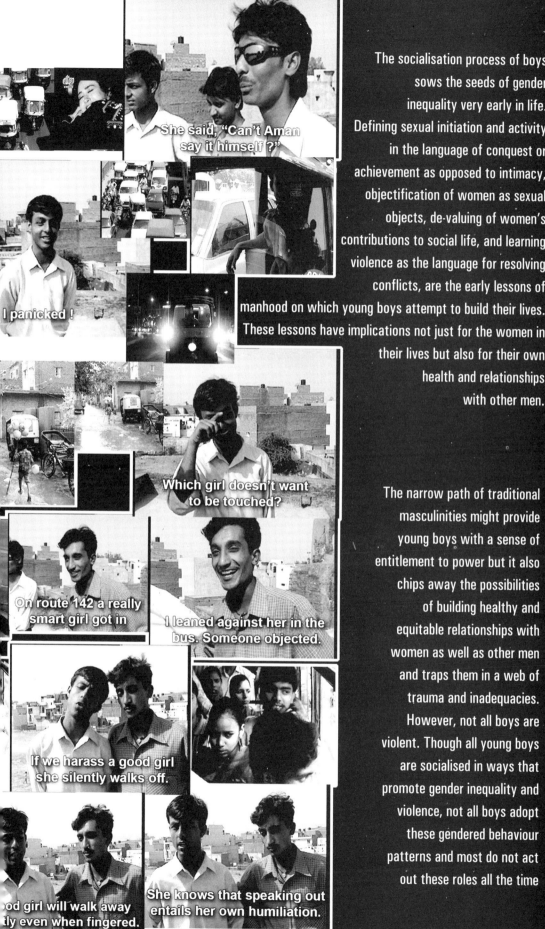

The socialisation process of boys sows the seeds of gender inequality very early in life. Defining sexual initiation and activity in the language of conquest or achievement as opposed to intimacy, objectification of women as sexual objects, de-valuing of women's contributions to social life, and learning violence as the language for resolving conflicts, are the early lessons of manhood on which young boys attempt to build their lives. These lessons have implications not just for the women in their lives but also for their own health and relationships with other men.

The narrow path of traditional masculinities might provide young boys with a sense of entitlement to power but it also chips away the possibilities of building healthy and equitable relationships with women as well as other men and traps them in a web of trauma and inadequacies. However, not all boys are violent. Though all young boys are socialised in ways that promote gender inequality and violence, not all boys adopt these gendered behaviour patterns and most do not act out these roles all the time

Munna, Aman and Tony are waiting in the line...
 when will their turn come...
when will they walk with a girl hand in hand...
They wait... and they dream... Eyes seeking, hands clammy.
Then they head towards a set of isolated tenements.
  For five rupees they can watch two video films.
It is an audience of all men, huddled together.
The blue light of the television playing on their faces...
 the glint of pleasure and secrecy in their eyes...

not a blink...
not a frame to be missed.

जुनून
डायजेस्ट

Pleasure almost always
 comes dancing with fear
 and anxiet

the memory of the first time
they masturbated haunts them...
Confusion, pleasure, anxiety...
twelve-year-olds discover
 strange sensations...
a tingling, the heady charge
and then the awful release...

a few drops of semen lost
 in many, many drops of bloo
gone down the drain...
 so they have been told...

they have all discussed
 the problem of weakness
and semen loss but
pleasure seems to be winning...

But then there are
 lurking fears of
what will happen by the
 time they get married...

will they still
 be able to perform
or will they become
 so weak that...

Masculine identities are marked by a sense of fragility and failure. It is this that leads to such great emphasis on 'performance' — the never-ending attempts at ensuring that expressions of male-ness meet certain prescribed norms.

The constant fear of failure to meet such norms — of sexual prowess, of being the undisputed family head, etc. — is often at the bottom of a great deal of masculine anxiety. Sexuality is the site of these anxieties and is tied up with such issues as being the ideal heterosexual male as well as the fear of non-heterosexual men. If masculinity were an indisputable — obvious, concrete — fact, rather than an identity always on the verge of being unravelled, then we would not require the constant efforts to convince ourselves otherwise. The varied attempts to establish and live up to masculine norms are indicative of their fragile nature.

"Masculinity is simultaneously a place in gender relations, the practices through which men and women engage that place in gender, and the effects of these practices in bodily experience, personality and culture."
Raewyn Connell

A discussion on Unpacking Masculinities

Connell has identified six themes that emerge from the study and activism around masculinities that can help us in better understanding the gendered behaviour patterns of men. Often the concept of the male sex role is utilised to discuss and explain gendered behaviour. However, it is an inadequate concept because it does not go beyond the social experience of learning the norms of conduct. It is also ill-equipped to discuss the diversity in the experience of masculinities and the power and economic dimension of gender.

Connell's work moves beyond the abstractions of the 'sex role' approach to a more concrete examination of how gender patterns are constructed and practised.

Classic Gents Cutting Styles

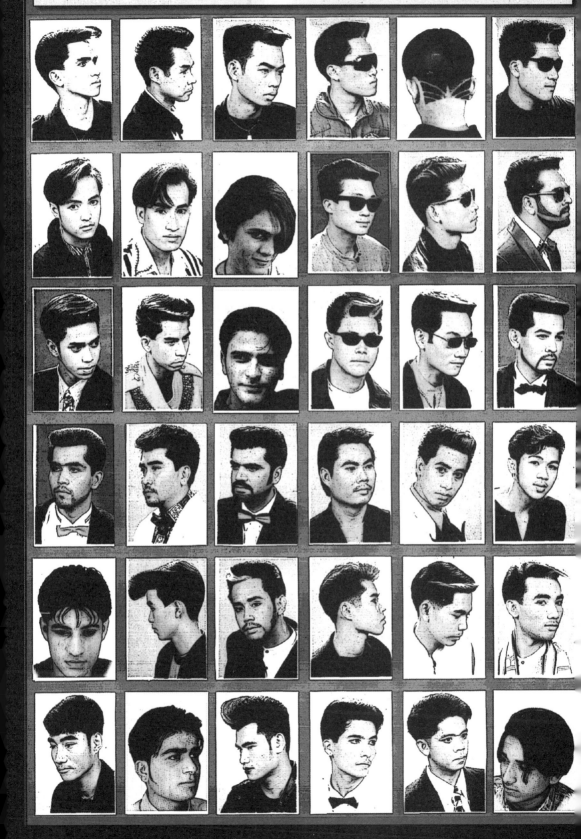

Multiple masculinities

There is no one universal pattern of masculinity. Social sciences research has clearly demonstrated the impossibility of talking about masculinity in the singular. Plurality of men's gendered behaviour patterns can be located in all cultures and through all historical periods. Different cultures and different periods of history construct masculinity differently.

For instance, if we were to take the phenomenon which gets associated the most with the term masculinity, that of violence, we can see that different cultures have different attitudes towards violence. Some cultures celebrate violence and make heroes of soldiers while others would go to extreme levels to eschew violence. The Dalai Lama's presence in India has given us an opportunity to see closely his brand of non-violence which is now celebrated all over the world as one of the most significant non-violent political movements.

Non-violence (*Ahimsa*) is the highest religious principle in Jainism and is the cardinal principle around which life is to be organised. It is the cornerstone of Jainism. Non-violence is the supreme religion (*Ahimsa parmo dharma*).

Tirthankaras in Jain literature stress: "Do not injure, abuse, oppress, enslave, insult, torment, torture, or kill any creature or living being."

The plurality of gender patterns is not restricted to different cultures alone. More than one kind of masculinity can be found within the same cultural setting. Within any community, worksite, neighbourhood or peer group, there are likely to be multiple understandings of masculinity and thereby of gender response and choice.

To put it simply, If we were to look at men around us, whether in an office, a classroom, a factory or any other work or institutional setting, they would be a fairly varied bunch as far as their gendered responses are concerned.

L. Elayaperumal, a Dalit leader, organised a mass movement in Puliangudi when Vadamalai, an ex-serviceman and son of the Dalit headman of the village, was tied to a tree and beaten up by caste Hindus for three days simply because he had entered the village, was well-dressed and wore a moustache "in violation of the village law".

Police authorities in Assam, India, are paying a monthly bonus to an officer who grows a moustache. One officer said "Having a big moustache is a symbol of masculinity and that helps you to excel in your professional duties as people are afraid to challenge you" (*Daily Telegraph*).

ony - There was this dialogue from Ajay
evgan's film, Hum Dil De chuke Sanam. He tells
is father that his wife loves someone else

Tony- His father asks
what kind of a man are
you? You cannot
control a woman?
He replies...It is not
right to exert control
over a defenseless
woman

Aman - He says Through force
I can possess her physically
but I cannot win her heart.

There
Tony - This is no masculinity in
beating a woman and exerting
control. I will not do it.

Munna - What is Masculinity then?

Aman - He was absolutely right

vi -   He should have taken out
s new leather belt and fixed her.

Munna - How can you beat your wife?

Ravi - The belt is always the best
solution for all problems.

Aman - In your thinking it might be
so but not in mine

Tony - However, you do have to show
who is the boss.

Munna - I would never beat my wife.

Ravi - You will never be able to control
her, maybe you will need my help! !

Tony - But how will you exert
your power then?

man - There must be other ways.

Munna - Why should you exert power?

Tony - I know who will wear
the pants in his house! !

Munna - You can say what you want
but I cannot beat my wife.

INDIAN POLICE GIVEN MOUSTACHE PAY

Police in a district in India's Madhya Pradesh state are being paid to grow moustaches because bosses believe it makes them command more respect.

Ten policemen in the northern state are already receiving 30 rupees every month for their efforts. Jhabua district police chief Mayank Jain told BBC News Online: "Moustaches are improving the personalities of our constables.

They are acquiring an aura of their own. They are creating a positive impression on the local people and getting a lot of respect."

"It takes time to keep a proper moustache. A good one has to take a turn near the angle of the upper lip," he added.

Men in rural India have traditionally sported impressive moustaches to assert their masculinity.

Hierarchy and Hegemony

But how do these different kinds of masculinities relate with each other?
Different forms of masculinities do not peacefully reside alongside each other.
They share a relationship which is fraught with tensions, struggles and alliances.

Most men as well as women have very interesting stories to narrate about the
pressures of performing or enacting certain gendered behaviour patterns that find
a peer or institutional acceptance, in schools, families or work sites. We know
that young boys in schools are put through a lot of pressure to appear strong and
physical, to be different from the so-called weaklings or "feminine" boys.

INDIAN ARMY PHYSICAL STANDARDS
The minimum physical standards have been laid down are region wise as follows :-

Region	State	Height cms	Weight kgs	Chest cms
Western Himalayan Region	J&K, HP, Punjab Hills (Area South & West of the Inter state Border between HP & Punjab and North and east of road of Mukerian, Hoshiarpur, Garhshankar, Ropar) Garhwal & Kumaon regions of Uttranchal.	166 163*	48	77
Eastern Himalayan Region	Nagaland, Manipur, Tripura, Mizoram, Meghalaya , Assam, Arunachal Pradesh , Sikkim and Hill Region of West Bengal (Darjeeling and Kalimpong Districts)	160 157*	48	77
Western Plains Region	Punjab, Haryana, Chandigarh , Delhi , Rajasthan and Western UP (Meerut and Agra Division)	170	50	77
Eastern Plains Region	Eastern UP, Bihar, West Bengal and Orissa	170	50	77
Central Region	Madhya Pradesh, Chattisgarh, Gujarat, Maharashtra, Dadar, Nagar-Haveli, Daman and Diu	168 167*	50	77
Southern Region	Andhra Pradesh, Karnataka Tamil Nadu, Kerala, Goa And Pondicherry	165	50	77

SPECIAL PHYSICAL STANDARDS
These are as follows :

	Height	Weight	Chest
Ladakhi	157	50	77
Gorkhas both Nepalese and Indians	160	48	77
Andaman, Nicobar Islands, Lakshadweep Group including Minicoy Settlers	165	50	77
Locals	155	50	77
Tribals of recognized areas	162	48	77
Brigade of the Guards	173	50	77
Med Arty	170	50	77
Corps Military Police	173	50	77
*Clerks GD/SKT	162	50	77

Soldier: Normal Physical Standards given
Tradesmen: Above minus 2 Cms height, 1 cm Chest and 2 Kgs weight.

FROM THE OFFICIAL WEBSITE OF THE INDIAN A

looking for someone who is educated, family oriented, wants to settle in the US. He should be tall, ...oing, adventurous and medium-built. Also someone who is understanding, loving, and open-minded.

First of all important thing.
ONLY JAT SIKH GUYS NEED TO RESPOND.
I am looking for person with whom I can live happily and enjoy my life. He should be open minded, understanding, and loyal to me. He should have patience and respect for elders and love for kids, should be helpful and softhearted. He should be postgraduate or holding professional degree.
ONLY FOR JAT SIKH FAMILIES. SHOULD BE AMERICAN CITIZEN. NO DOWRY.

...ee their bodies!
See their bodies!

This is Aslam ...

See his thighs...

...they are like tree trunks

He should hold a strong character, honest, polite and caring. He should be smart yet simple and respect elders. He should be from well known professional/artistic or business family. Hindu and hindi speaking.

...le non-trimmer, tee-age up to 30, Height ...um 5'7" gurmukh ...contact

...cutive personality ...ller, sound health ALLAH fearing manners three ... brothers. Three ...ll married already ...urately settled well. ...ther alive.

Diya is a homely, smart and well-educated girl. We are looking for a guy who is educated and well settled either in family business or professionally.

I am a 25 year old man based in Mumbai. Looking for well built, hairless / less hair / hairy handsome men with rough and tough personality in handling me... very very manly actions..

I am a very self motivated, generous, focussed & strong willed person. I strongly believe & follow the principles of simple... He is confident, smart, fun-loving, caring, extrovert, witty person having positive attitude towards life...Country Lover... OR Bhartiya Yodhdha.. Or say to me... Indian Warrior... Sunder man aur sunder soch hi sunderta ki sab se paheli nishaani hoti hai...About me if I were to give even a slight bit of introduction it would take more than 5 to 10 pages...

"The form of masculinity which is culturally dominant in a given setting is called 'hegemonic masculinity'. Hegemonic signifies a position of cultural authority and leadership, not total dominance; other forms of masculinity persist alongside. Also, the hegemonic masculinity need not be the most common form of masculinity but rather the most visible. Hegemonic masculinity is hegemonic not just in relation to other masculinities, but in relation to the gender order as a whole. It is an expression of the privilege men collectively have over women. The hierarchy of masculinities is an expression of the unequal shares in that privilege held by different groups of men."
Raewyn Connell

...n a Textile Designer. I am ...or a very good looking, tall, ...ucated and well-settled ...rahmin guy, who has strong ...decent family background ...espectable position in the ...believe in GOD, Speed, Time ...ey.

I am interested in someone who is ambitious, fun loving, open-minded, understanding and caring. I am looking for someone who I can trust and be open with, someone to share life's experiences with.... both good and bad times. Sense of humour, sincerity and dependability are qualities I am looking for. who is currently handling respectable and responsible position in a MNC / Business Family. who have high goals and Ambition in life and who is honest, caring and loving.

...uy who ...r love, ...for love ...will die ...am loo- ...partner ...d who ...s me ...th care ...ads his ...me. I ...to give ...uch of ...n every ...corner ...t tease, ...soft & ...n.

Looking for guys with professional degree. Should be smart, aff-luent, easy going, and please respond with pic!

How is he ...ooking?

Are you enjoying the sight?

Prefers guy to be macho man non-feminine decent well mannered.... Good built n healthy n who maintains body neat n hygenic....

Hi I am a 22year old looking 4 the man of my dreams. I am looking for somebody who is a perfect blend of good looks and brains...smartness and intelligence with a good sense of humour in a man really turns me on...and definitely a good family background.... and above all a self made man.

Sex: Male. Attracted to: Male. Seeking a relationship for: You know what! Background /Ethnicity: North Indian. Turn ons: Tall, strong men. Body hair: Smooth. Stature: Tall. Body type description: I am muscular hairy hand-some. Preferred body type(s): Tall, muscular, smooth, short hair, sharp features

I want a good looking, hand-some husband, from a good family. Should be economic-ally sound and from Kolkata. He should be tall.

Girl from a very high class family seeks boy from a good family.

...Indian, but I was born and raised in the U.S. I want an educated, ...e, cultured, and respectable man. Someone who is caring and considerate ...I am interested in more of a long-term relationship. I am only looking for ...ducated man who is raised in USA. Men from India please don't reply.

A FATHER WAS WORRIED THAT HIS FAMILY BUSINESS WOULD BE DESTROYED BY THE INFIGHTING AMONGST HIS SONS.

ONE DAY HE GATHERED THEM TOGETHER AND GAVE EACH A STICK. HE THEN ASKED THEM TO BREAK IT.

Collective masculinities

Though we tend to talk more about gender conduct as an individual trait, and thus describe behaviour patterns as "masculine" or "feminine", there is a collective aspect of masculinities that often gets ignored. The collective articulation of masculinities is best exemplified by institutions like the army, police, schools, gangs, corporations, factories as also in the arena of sports. All these institutions nurture, harness and unleash a collective aggressive masculinity that is created organisationally by the structures of these institutions, by their systems of training and their hierarchy of levels and rewards.

THIS THEY DID EASILY. NOW, HE ASKED THEM TO TIE THE STICKS TOGETHER AND TRY AGAIN.

THEY TRIED WITH ALL THEIR STRENGTH, BUT THE BUNDLE PROVED IMPOSSIBLE TO BREAK.

COLLECTIVE MASCULINITY MAKES BUSINESS SENSE

too quiet

not aggressive enough

cannot lead

bad attitude (and tick appropriate answer)

no initiative

S.N.	Question	Reply
1	I am part of social groups	☑Always ☐Often ☐Sometimes ☐Rarely ☐
2	I like informal social activities	☐Always ☑Often ☐Sometimes ☐Rarely ☐
3	I'm not a loner	☐Always ☐Often ☑Sometimes ☐Rarely ☐Never
4	I like close relationships with people	☐Always ☑Often ☐Sometimes ☐Rarely ☐Never
5	I join social organisations if I have a chance	☐Always ☐Often ☑Someti... ☐ver
6	Other people strongly influence my actions	☐Always ☐Often ☑So...
7	I allow other people to decide what to do	☐Always ☐Often ☐So...
8	...personal relationships with people	☑Always ☐Often ☐Son...
9	...re included in my plans	☐Always ☐Often ☐Someti...
10	...d by people	☐Always ☑Often ☐Sometimes ☐Rarely ☐Never
11	...people around me	☐A... ...etimes ☐Rarely ☐Never
12	...close and personal with people	...times ☐
13	I join people who do things together	...mes ☐
14	I let other people control my actions	...mes ☐
15	I try to be with people	...times ☐R... ☐Never
16	I try to participate in group activities.	☐Always ☑... ...Sometimes ☐Rarely ☐Never

not presentable enough

not a company man

very casually dressed

bad english

Now answer according to;

17	I am friendly with people	... ...Some ☐Few ☐Noone
18	Other people decide what I do	... ...Some ☑T... ☐Noone
19	...with people are reserved and cool	... ...Some ☐Few ☐Noone
...	...charge	... ☑Some ☐Few ☐Noone
...	...tionships with people	☐All people ☑Majority ☐Some ☐Few ☐Noone
...	...trol my actions	☐All people ☐Majority ☐Some ☑Few ☐
25	I act reserved with people	☐All people ☐Majority ☑Some ☐Few
...	People can lead me easily	☐All people ☐Majority ☐Some ☑Few
28	I let p... ...to do things	☐All people ☑Majority ☐Some ☐Few
29	I let ...d personal with me	☑All people ☐Majority ☐Some ☐Few
30	I infl... ...actions of other people	☐All people ☑Majority ☐Some ☐Few
32	I like ...e towards me	☑All people ☐Majority ☐Some ☐Few ☐Noone
33	I take ...m with people	☐All people ☐Majority ☑Some ☐Few
34	I like people ...include me in their activities	☐All people ☑Majority ☐Some ☐F...
36	I like people to do things the way I want them done	☐All people ☐Majority ☑Some ☐Fe...
38	I like people to act friendly towards me	☑All people ☐Majority ☐Some ☐Few ☐Noone

poor projection skills

sloppy and untidy

not a team player

must speak up

not smart

Now answer according to;

41	I try to dominate when I am with people	☑Always ☐Often ☐Sometimes ☐Rarely ☐Never
42	I let people invite me to do things	☐Always ☑Often ☐Sometimes ☐Rarely ☐Never
43	I let people act close towards me	☑Always ☐Often ☐Sometimes ☐Rare...
44	I have other people to do things I want done	☑Always ☐Often ☐Sometimes ☐Ra...
46	I like people to act cool and distant towards me	☐Always ☑Often ☐Sometimes ☐Ra...
47	I like to influence strongly other people's actions	☐Always ☑Often ☐Sometimes ☐Ra...
...	...ople to include me in their activities	☐Always ☑Often ☐Sometimes ☐Ra...
...	...ople to act close and personal with me	☐Always ☑Often ☐Sometimes ☐Ra...
...	...ge of things when I am with people	☐Always ☑Often ☐Sometimes ☐Rarely ☐
...	...articipate in group activities	☐Always ☑Often ☐Sometimes ☐Rarely ☐Never
...	...ople to act distant towards me	☐Always ☐Of... ...☑Rarely ☐Never
...	...ke to get my way with people	☐Always ☑... ...arely ☐Never
54	I take charge of things when I am with people	☑Always ☐... ...rely ☐Never

not tall enough

not a go getter

must learn to think on feet

no clarity of goals

not a winner

Masculinities or for that matter any gendered behaviour pattern do not exist prior to social behaviour, either as bodily states or fixed personalities. Rather, masculinities come into existence as people act, as they make choices or as they perform. They are accomplished in everyday conduct or organisational life, as patterns of social practice.

Gender is about making a choice, consciously or unconsciously, it is about doing in everyday life. Violence, for instance, is not a fixed masculine characteristic but rather a resource to construct particular kinds of masculinities.

"Masculinity is not a stable form of gender behaviour but a state which has to be constantly striven for and is not a neutral condition that comes out spontaneously through biological maturation but rather a precarious or artificial state that must be won at all odds." (Shekhar Sheshadri)

Active Constructions

MALE KARNEG

SUCCESSFUL MEN HAVE AMBITION.

THEY HAVE ENTHUSIASM, COMMITMENT, AND PRIDE THEY HAVE SELF-DISCIPLIN THEY'RE WILLING TO DO WHATEVER IT TAKES TO GET THE JOB DONE.

Successful Mer Make Decision

Decisions aren't pu off or delayed, they're made now!

Successful Men can leac

They have positive, outgoing personalities They surround themselves with peop who offer them help, support, and encouragement. They are leaders.

"Asking 'who ought to be the boss' is like asking 'who ought to be the tenor in the quartet?' Obviously, the man who can sing tenor."

Henry Ford

Successful Men Have a Dream.

They have a well-defined purpose.
They have a definite goal.
They know what they want.
They produce results, not excuses.

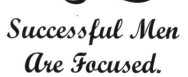

Successful Men Are Focused.

They concentrate on their main goals and objectives. They don't get sidetracked.

Successful Men Look for Solutions to Problems.

They're opportunity minded. When they see opportunities they take advantage of them.

Results justify the means.

Because they enable you to achieve your goals.

SUCCESSFUL MEN TAKE RESPONSIBILITY FOR THEIR ACTIONS.

THEY DON'T MAKE EXCUSES.
THEY DON'T BLAME OTHERS.
THEY DON'T WHINE AND COMPLAIN.

Successful Men Are Strongly Motivated Towards Achievement.

They take great satisfaction in accomplishing a task.

Successful Men Are Self-reliant.

They have the skills, talents, and training that are needed.

SUCCESSFUL MEN DRAW PEOPLE TO THEM.

Because these people want to work with them,
do business with them, and be with them.

Successful Men Know How to Get Things Done.

They do the things that need to be done, not just the things they like to do. They are willing to commit themselves to getting the job done.

I WANT TO BE LIKE HIM

One of the key reasons why masculinities are unstable is that they are not simple, homogenous patterns. Patterns of masculinities often reveal desires and logics that are contradictory. Masculinities almost always have multiple possibilities. The complexity of desires and emotions is important to observe and understand because they are the resources of tension and change in gender patterns.

Internal

Complexity

This creature
We know as man
Is one big chaos
O desires and thoughts
Even when lonely
He's never alone
For in his breast
Lies hidden
A tumultous crowd.

Ghalib

DYnamics

From the fact that different masculinities exist in different cultures and historical periods we can conclude that masculinities are able to change. The layering of masculinities displays the sources of change and within the hierarchy of masculinities lie the motives for change.

The dynamics of masculinities refers to the fact that particular forms of masculinities are composed historically and may also get decomposed, contested and replaced. There is an active politics of gender in everyday life. Sometimes it takes the shape of a public expression but more often it is local and limited. However, there is always a process of contestation and change, and in some cases this becomes conscious and deliberate.

An episode surrounding the Khudai Khidmatgars and Khan Abdul Ghaffar Khan, or Frontier Gandhi as he was fondly called, from the history of the Indian sub-continent exemplifies the dynamic nature of masculinities and the possibilities of change.

By 1929, Khan and his band of red shirts had become fervent Gandhians and the creed of non-violence, it is reported, sharply brought down the blood feuds amongst the Pathans. By May 1930 the number of Khudai Khidmatgars had risen to 50,000 from 500 in a mere six months. The arrest of Badshah Khan and other leaders led to a massive upsurge in Peshawar with crowds confronting armoured cars and defying intensive firing for three hours at the Kissakhani bazaar. A platoon of Garhwal rifles composed of non-Muslims refused to fire at the Muslim crowd , declaring that they would not fire on their unarmed brethren... the platoon of course was court martialled later. The latter part of 1930s saw protests and incursions from various Pathan tribal areas but unlike the earlier raids these did not witness any violence and looting of villages and with moving simplicity raised demands for the release of Badshah Khan, Malang Baba and Inquilab. (Sumit Sarkar)

It was under Chandra Singh Garhwali's leadership that the soldiers of the Garhwal Rifles refused to fire upon the demonstrators.

GREAT MEN OF INDIA

Mahatma Gandhi

Chandra Shekhar Azad

Akbar

Jyotirao Phule

Maharana Pratap

Kabir

Bhagat Singh

Prithvi Raj Chauhan

Raja Rammohan Roy

Indira Gandhi

Rabindranath Tagore

Shivaji

Guru Nanak

Guru Gobind Singh

Rani Lakshmi Bai

Amitabh Bachchan

Swami Vivekananda

Pundit Nehru

Aurobindo Ghosh

Khan Abdul Ghaffar Khan

Baba Ambedkar

Dev Anand

Subhas Chandra Bose

Tipu Sultan

DEFINITION ?!@

One issue that almost always crops up when we discuss masculinities is of definitions. HOW do you define masculinities? Several definitions have been offered that attempt to locate masculinities within the twin concepts of power and violence. However, it has been argued that most definitions of masculinity are simplistic and rest on rather static notions of gender identity. The issue is further problematised by the existence of what is termed 'female masculinities', which refers to the practice of gender behaviour patterns by women that are traditionally associated with men. Thus, it is difficult to restrict the concept of masculinities to the male body. Realising the difficulties of offering a definition the effort in social science has been to map masculinites as actual patterns of conduct or representations.

Connell argues that however problematic the concept of masculinities, we always presuppose a distinction between men and women. We do need to comprehend in language men's and women's involvement in the domain of gender and thereby distinguish conduct which is oriented to or shaped by that domain from other forms of social conduct. Masculinities may not be the perfect term to provide an exclusive understanding or exploration of men's gendered behaviour patterns but it remains the most useful term available to us at present.

Rani Lakshmibai

Rani Channamma

Rani Avantibai

Rani Durgavati

Jhalkaribai

FROM THE MOUTHS OF THE BUNDELA HARBOLAS WE HAVE HEARD THE STORY

BRAVELY SHE FOUGHT AS A MAN,

SHE WAS THE QUEEN OF JHANSI

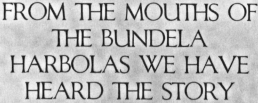

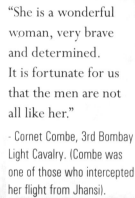

"She is a wonderful woman, very brave and determined. It is fortunate for us that the men are not all like her."

- Cornet Combe, 3rd Bombay Light Cavalry. (Combe was one of those who intercepted her flight from Jhansi).

Inki gaatha chhod, chaley hum Jhansi key maidanon mein,
Jahan khadi hai Lakshmibai mard bani mardanon mein,
Lieutenant Walker aa pohoncha, aagey bada jawanon mein,
Rani ney talwaar kheench li, hua dhandh asmanon mein.
Zakhmi hokar Walker bhaga, usey ajab hairani thi,
Bundeley Harbolon key munh hamney suni kahani thi,
Khoob ladi mardani woh to Jhansi wali Rani thi.

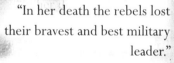

"In her death the rebels lost their bravest and best military leader."

- Regimental history of the 8th Hussars. (The 8th Hussars are most probably the unit responsible for her death.)

The word most often used in the context of masculinities is power. Most often masculinity is defined as the experiencing of power. However, Michael Kimmel defines masculinity as more about the experience of **entitlement to power** in that a man's experience of power depends on where he stands on the social ladder in terms of class, caste, sexual orientation, physical appearance, the region he comes from, etc. This has important implications because it extends the theoretical boundaries of understanding masculinities beyond men as **custodians and wielders** of power to men negotiating often **contradictory** flows of power and their sense of entitlement to power.

This is not to suggest that men have no power. Men as a group have power over women and over other men by virtue of class, caste, race, sexual orientation, etc., however, the experience is never absolute. If on one axis, vis-à-vis his wife, a man experiences power, he could experience powerlessness on another axis, if, say, he is lower in the caste hierarchy than the men of the dominant caste.

A survey of Fortune 500 CEO height in 2005 revealed that they were on average 6 feet tall, which is 3 inches taller than the average American man. Fully 30% of these CEOs were 6 feet 2 inches tall or more; in comparison only 3.9% of the overall United States population is of this height. Equally significantly, similar surveys have uncovered that less than 3% of CEOs were below 5'7" in height, and that 90% of CEOs are of above average height. Subjectively, many short persons report they are not taken seriously in the work place or by their peers because of their smaller stature. Objectively, surveys of attitudes do reveal that people both perceive and treat people of shorter stature as inferior, and that the significant economic differentials are the direct result of height discrimination.

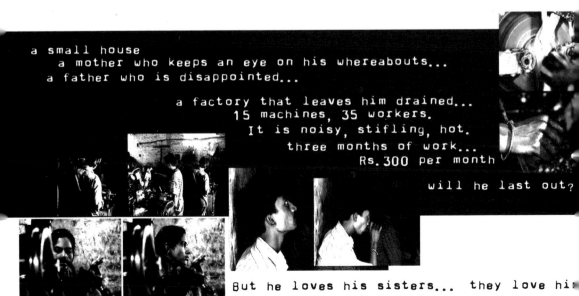

a small house
   a mother who keeps an eye on his whereabouts...
a father who is disappointed...

      a factory that leaves him drained...
         15 machines, 35 workers.
         It is noisy, stifling, hot.
            three months of work...
               Rs.300 per month

                        will he last out?

But he loves his sisters... they love hi

hey wash his clothes...

Munna wants to breathe

who's bothered ?

Why should we be bothered about masculinities?

We do need to broaden our understanding of gender and till now the research, at least in South Asia, has concentrated on women's lives and histories when speaking of gender. This could be the sole purpose of research — to increase our knowledge about a field which remains an area of darkness.

A more practical reason for looking closely at masculinities is that they have been identified as a rather toxic part of our social life. Violence, ill health, accidents, high levels of injury outside the home, conflict, rape, domestic violence are all patterns of behaviour which have been associated with men.

A study of masculinities could also demonstrate the possibilities of change. We know that masculinities are not static and are locked in a perpetual state of conflict. Greater insights into these conflicts could provide us with indicators of change.

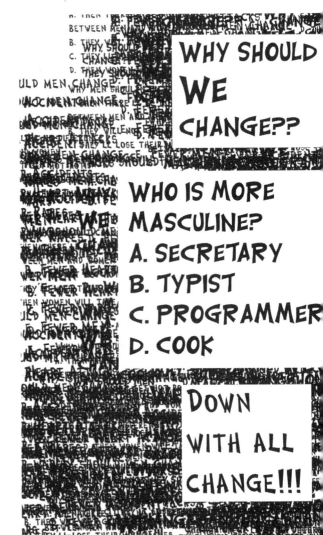

WHY SHOULD WE CHANGE??

WHO IS MORE MASCULINE?
A. SECRETARY
B. TYPIST
C. PROGRAMMER
D. COOK

DOWN WITH ALL CHANGE!!!

DOWN
WITH
CHANGE

WHY SHOULD MEN CHANGE
A. FEWER ACCIDENTS
B. FEWER HEART ATTACKS
C. FEWER RAPES
D. FEWER WARS
E. FEWER MEN

CHANGE
CAUSES
CHAOS

WHY SHOULD MEN
CHANGE ??
THEY SHOULDN'T !!

WHY MEN SHOULDN'T CHANGE
A. THEN THERE'LL BE NO DIFFERENCE
BETWEEN MEN AND WOMEN
B. THEY WILL NOT GET HOT ROTIS
C. THEY'LL LOSE THEIR MOUSTACHES
D. THEN WOMEN WILL TAKE OVER

*It has been a while
Since my self became
displeased with me
And left.
What remains with me
Is an empty shell,
That is the companion
Of the dying walls of
this old house.*

Shiv Kumar Batalvi

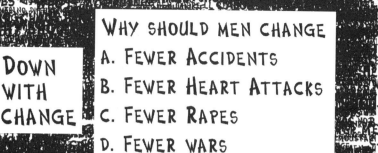

everyone whispers that the sky looks different
it is just not the same, they say...
Munna worries
the past he doesn't know...
the present leaves him confused
the future?
should he make of it?
Aman, Tony and Ravi too are confused...
there is no one to talk to

Most often the question of why men should change is answered, quite justifiably, by citing the immense price women have to pay because of the existing gender inequalities and the violence women have to face. This seems a valid enough answer because we want to build a world free of gender inequalities and oppression.

But **why** should men participate in such an exercise? Why should they change a behaviour pattern which has been honed by centuries of patriarchal organising of our social, economic and political lives and privileges the masculine?

The key to answering the question why men should change lies in understanding the nature of relationship between masculinities and power.

a BOX on Patriarchy

"Patriarchy in its wider definition means the manifestation and institutionalisation of male dominance over women and children in the family; and the extension of male dominance over women in society in general. It implies that men hold power in all the important institutions of society and that women are deprived of access to such power. It does not imply that women are either totally powerless or totally deprived of rights, influences and resources. One of the most challenging tasks of Women's History is to trace with precision the various forms and modes in which patriarchy appears historically, the shifts and changes in its structure and function, and the adaptations it makes to female pressure and demands.

Patriarchy as a system is historical; it has a beginning in history. If that is so, it can be ended by historical process."

The Creation of Patriarchy By Gerda Lerner

Munna loses himself
        in the image...
A darkened hall
the bright screen
     several eyes
       unblinking

    he cries
    laughs
    fights...
    and in the end he wins...
          he also gets the girl

 you know what it is like to be at the top of the world?
supreme...
       a man

hy does this magic ever end?
Why does the world come rushing in?   So harsh...   so mundane...

I'M FINE, THANK YOU.
OK.   I'M OK.   I'M OK.
I'M GREAT.   I'M OK.   I'M GREAT   GREAT.
GREAT.   I'M FINE.   I'M OK.   I'M OK.
I'M FINE. OK.   I'M OK.   I'M FINE. OK.   I'M OK.
I'M FINE. I'M GREAT.   I'M FINE.   I'M OK.
I'M GREAT.   I'M OK.
I'M FINE, THANK YOU. I'M GREAT.
I'M FINE.   I'M FINE.   I'M OK.
I'M OK.   I'M OK.
M OK.   I'M GREAT. OK.
I'M OK. I'M FINE.   I'M OK.   I'M FINE.
I'M   I'M OK. I'M OK. I'M OK. FINE.   I'M OK.
I'M GREAT.   FINE. I'M OK.
I'M GREAT. I'M OK. I'M GREAT.
I'M FINE.
I'M OK.   I'M FINE.   I'M OK.
I'M FINE, THANK YOU.
I'M OK. OK.
I'M OK.
I'M FINE.
I'M GREAT.

I'M FINE.

Yesterday, I was collecting words.

One was up there, sitting in the bo tree,
Another was in the banyan.
One was wandering in my street,
Another was lying in the earthen jar.
A green word lay in the fields,
A black one was eating flesh.
A blue word was flying
With a grain of the sun in its beak.
Every single thing in this world looks like a word to me.
The words of eyes,
The words of hands.
But I do not understand words I hear from a mouth.
I can only read words.
I can only read words.

Shiv Kumar Batalvi

The Hero
by Rabindranath Tagore

Mother, let us imagine we are travelling, and passing through a strange and dangerous country. You are riding in a palanquin and I am trotting by you on a red horse. It is evening and the sun goes down. The waste of Joradighilies wan and grey before us. The land is desolate and barren. You are frightened and thinking—"I know not where we have come to." I say to you, "Mother, do not be afraid." The meadow is prickly with spiky grass, and through it runs a narrow broken path. There are no cattle to be seen in the wide field; they have gone to their village stalls. It grows dark and dim on the land and sky, and we cannot tell where we are going. Suddenly you call me and ask me in a whisper, "What light is that near the bank?" Just then there bursts out a fearful yell, and figures come running towards us. You sit crouched in your palanquin and repeat the names of the gods in prayer. The bearers, shaking in terror, hide themselves in the thorny bush. I shout to you, "Don't be afraid, mother. I am here." With long sticks in their hands and hair all wild about their heads, they come nearer and nearer. I shout, "Have a care, you villains! One step more and you are dead men." They give another terrible yell and rush forward. You clutch my hand and say, "Dear boy, for heaven's sake, keep away from them." I say, "Mother, just you watch me." Then I spur my horse for a wild gallop, and my sword and buckler clash against each other. The fight becomes so fearful, mother, that it would give you a cold shudder could you see it from your palanquin. Many of them fly, and a great number are cut to pieces. I know you are thinking, sitting all by yourself, that your boy must be dead by this time. But I come to you all stained with blood, and say, "Mother, the fight is over now." You come out and kiss me, pressing me to your heart, and you say to yourself, "I don't know what I would do if I hadn't my boy to escort me." A thousand useless things happen day after day, and why couldn't such a thing come true by chance? It would be like a story in a book. My brother would say, "Is it possible? I always thought he was so delicate!" Our village people would all say in amazement, "Was it not lucky that the boy was with his mother?"

Men should change because the power position they seek through their lives is never going to be absolute. In fact, in the march towards achieving the grade of 'men' they are going to lose touch with many 'human' emotions and construct for themselves a web of trauma and pain from which there is most often no exit.

How do we develop a language which assists men in making the journey women have made? The women's movement generated a language which helped women's subjective experience of being women become an objective, collective experience. Can we dream of a similar experience for men?

Michael Kimmel has argued that the subjective experience of the contradictory nature of power flow has to become an objective reality for men. Only then can we hope for a real dismantling of the patriarchal gender system.

Words... words... words... why do they seem so elusive... there is so much Munna could have said that day...

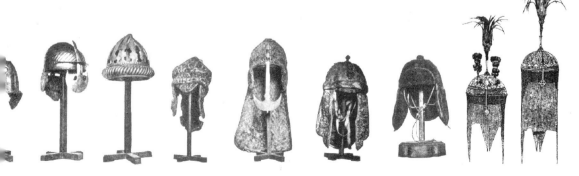

```
...why do words always escape
        him when he needs their
protection the most...

    or is it that silence
                is safe...

    pushed to the wall...
        unable to understand
    feeling persecuted...
            lost... defeated

he then picks up all the
        little stones of silence
    and builds a wall...

        But is he safe inside?
    For how long?

Will he survive or suffer...
            even more
```

To achieve change, however, is easier said than done. It is not easy to talk to men about changing.

The answers probably lie in the experience of the women's movement. A sharing of experiences by men to draw out other men could be a beginning.

There is need to evolve a language and discover words which are specific to the experience of men just as the women's movement evolved its own language.

We have often heard the demand for the breaking of silence, but this is mostly in the context of women. It is equally critical for men to break their silence.

This silence, this inability to be self-reflexive, to put words to feelings, is, in the long run extremely dangerous because this silence represents a failure of self-comprehension, an inability to make oneself the subject of discourse.

And unless we do that we will not change. When we don't know our subjective self where is the question of change?

Masculinity as a gender system today stands problematised because of the pressures from the women's movement. This might be difficult to imagine now but sooner or later, men as a group will thank the women's movement for having pushed them on a journey of self-discovery.

I don't know what happened to me that day.
I suddenly felt these warm tears
flowing down my cheeks.
I wept and I wept..

Aman, Tony and Ravi
kept asking me but
I had no answers.

Don't cry like this,
I too will start crying.

He is mad!

What could I say?
I didn't know why I was crying.
Something just snapped.
Maybe it had something to do with...

I really don't know.
I was really surprised when
Aman said
he also cries sometimes...

In a strange way I felt happy...
I wasn't alone...
Otherwise I would have said I was fine

What is he
crying about?

You turned out to
be a real softie

He is large hearted, that's
why he's crying

The large hearted swall[o]
their tears

Men don't cry.
Girls do that.

Men don't cry in
front of others.

Whenever I need to cry
I do so at night alone.